The Ethiopian Wolf
Hope at the Edge of Extinction

First published in the United States in 2013 by Lobelia Press
San Francisco, CA

Edited by Jacqueline S. Volin

Images from this book are available for licensing through the Ethiopian Wolf Project image collection (www.EthiopianWolfProject.com) or directly from the photographers.
William Burrard-Lucas | www.Burrard-Lucas.com
Rebecca R Jackrel | www.RebeccaJackrel.com

Printed in China on FSC-Certified Paper using DIC vegetable based inks

Cover Page Image: *Alarm Call*, Ethiopian Wolf (Canis simensis), © 2011 Will Burrard-Lucas
Back Page Image: *The Better to Hear You With*, Ethiopian Wolf (Canis simensis), © 2011 Rebecca R Jackrel

ISBN-13: 978-0-9815813-1-6
Library of Congress Control Number: 2013901848

To
Nat, Lee and April

Will Burrard-Lucas

Rebecca R Jackrel

Jaymi Heimbuch

The Ethiopian Wolf
Hope at the Edge of Extinction

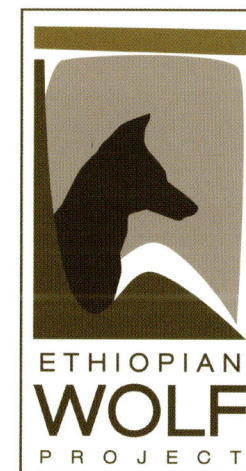

ETHIOPIAN
WOLF
PROJECT

Lobelia Press
San Francisco, CA

"Photographers deal in things which are
continuously vanishing and when they have vanished
there is no contrivance on earth
which can make them come back again."

Henri Cartier-Bresson
The Decisive Moment

Contents

INTRODUCTION

The world is shrinking day by day, or at least it feels that way. Google has mapped more than 75 percent of inhabited areas including every continent—even Antarctica—and more is added to Google Earth every two weeks. Meanwhile, the human population has more than doubled in the last fifty years. According to the United Nations Population Fund, there are now seven billion people on the planet. Our massive population is using resources faster than the earth can replenish them. Deforestation, pollution, habitat destruction, desertification, climate change, invasive species, overexploitation of resources, urbanization, overfishing, and disease are all factors in a significant loss of biodiversity worldwide. Every second, a slice of rainforest the size of a football field disappears forever. Five out of every hundred people on the earth suffer from a lack of access to clean water. According to the International Union for Conservation of Nature (IUCN) Red List, one out of four mammal species, one in eight bird species, and one in three amphibian species are at risk of extinction.

As disturbing as these statistics are, it's not time to give up hope, not when dedicated conservationists are fighting to protect the species and places they love so passionately. These dedicated men and women know that in order to save a species, they must protect its ecosystem as a whole. In so doing, conservationists are also helping humankind, because we depend on healthy ecosystems as well, to provide us with medicines, regulate climate, prevent erosion so we can continue to grow food, and give us clean air to breathe and clean water to drink. Thanks to dedicated conservationists and scientists, recovery efforts for damaged ecosystems and threatened species are under way in countries all across the globe.

One such conservation biologist is Professor Claudio Sillero-Zubiri. Upon meeting Claudio, one is immediately struck by his passion for the endangered Ethiopian wolf and the Ethiopian highlands. When he speaks of the wolves, he speaks as a proud father would of his children. Fewer than 450 of these wolves remain on the planet, and Claudio can't save them all on his own. He has an entire team working year round to combat the threats to this enigmatic species, and that costs money. Raising money takes visibility, and that is where the conservation wildlife photographer can help.

Jacques-Yves Cousteau said, "People protect what they love and love what they understand." Photography provides access to and greater understanding of species such as the Ethiopian wolf. Only a relative handful of people will be able to travel to the Ethiopian highlands to see the wolves firsthand, but through photography we can bring the wolves into people's homes, we can engage the armchair traveler and the couch conservationist. Even from a distance, viewers can help protect the subjects of these photographs.

With the goal of just such engagement in mind, the Ethiopian Wolf Project was born. In February 2011, wildlife photographer Rebecca Jackrel traveled to the Bale Mountains with Professor Sillero on a scouting trip. They were joined by thirteen people from five countries, a diverse group united by a passion for conservation and for wild canids. Claudio introduced the group to the Afroalpine region and the amazing creatures that are dependent on this fragile habitat. After returning home, Rebecca teamed up with fellow wildlife photographer Will Burrard-Lucas and together they formed the Ethiopian Wolf Project.

That November, armed with the scientific knowledge provided by Claudio Sillero and the local contacts made on the scouting trip, Rebecca and Will set out for the Bale Mountains to begin the work of documenting, through photography, the story of the Ethiopian wolf. Because the successful rearing of the next generation of wolf pups is paramount to the survival of the species, Rebecca and Will spent five weeks at the height of the wolf breeding season working with local wolf watchers and monitors to capture an intimate view of the lives of the wolves as they raise their family. Through their combined efforts, they hope to bring awareness of the Ethiopian wolf to a wide audience and build support for the ongoing conservation efforts to protect the species.

As long as there are people who continue to care, continue to fight for the conservation of biodiversity, there is hope for the future not only of endangered species but also for all humankind. We hope that you will enjoy this book, that our images will help you create a connection with the beautiful highland wolves of Africa and inspire you to get involved. In the words of David Orr, the Paul Sears Distinguished Professor of Environmental Studies and Politics at Oberlin College, "When we heal the earth, we heal ourselves."

The photographers exploring the Sanetti Plateau from horseback. Bale Mountains National Park, Ethiopia.

Map of Ethiopia showing the six mountain ranges containing populations of Ethiopian Wolves.

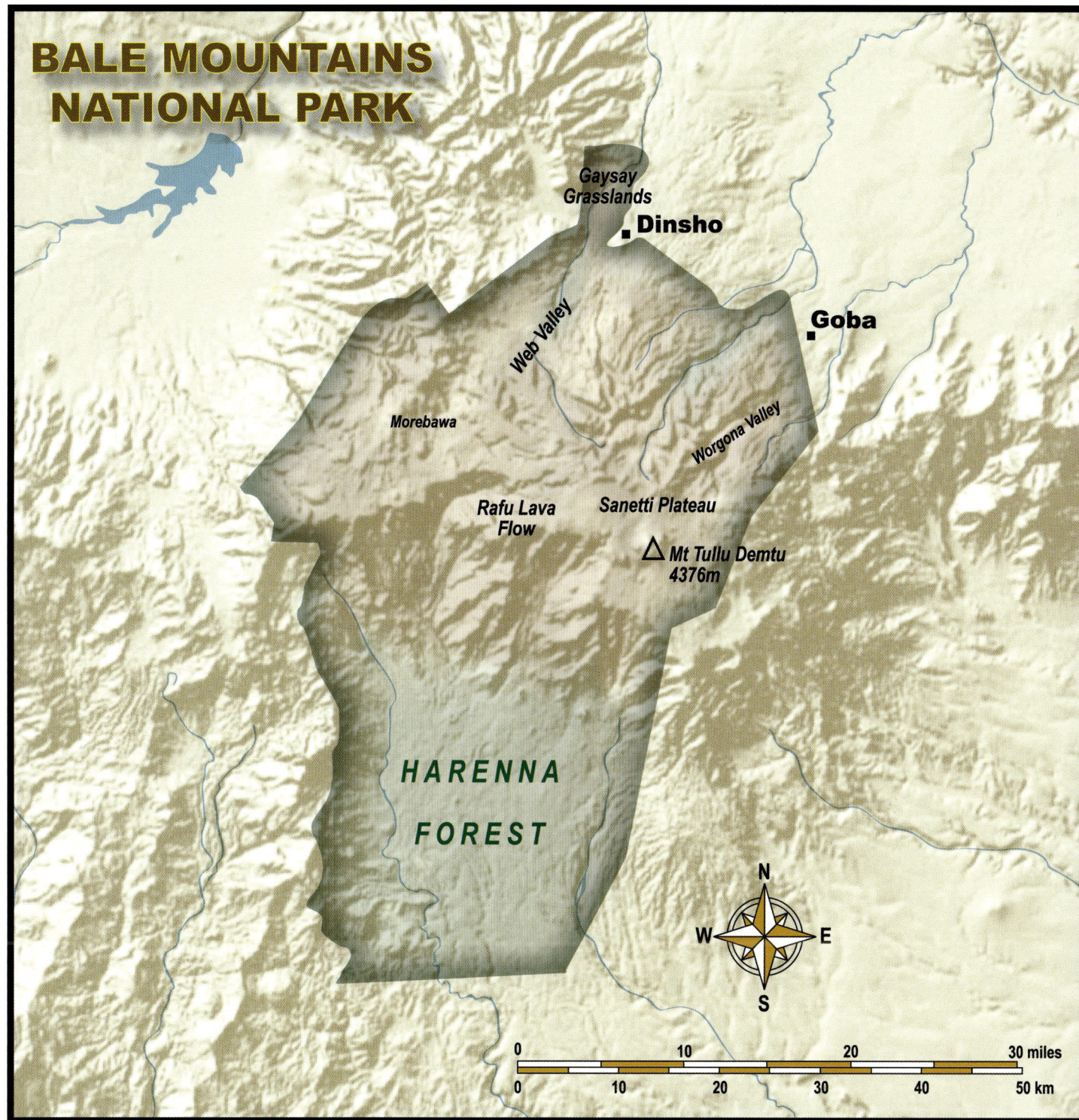

Map of the Bale Mountains National Park showing areas important to the Ethiopian Wolf.

A member of the Alandu pack crosses a stream into Meggity territory in the Web Valley. This remote and inaccesible area is one of the last remaining strongholds of the Ethiopian wolf. It is superb wolf habitat due to the very high density of rodents it supports. However, even here the wolves are seriously threatened by human encroachment and diseases passed on by domestic dogs.

Following pages: Sunrise is a spectacular sight in the Web Valley. As the hue of the sky shifts from purple to orange, the warmth of the rising sun begins to burn the frost from the shrubs creating low, clinging fog to add mystery and drama to the beautiful landscape. If you were a member of the Tarura pack, this view would be yours every morning.

Though they may be solitary hunters, the wolves are intensely social creatures, and cuddling together for warmth in the cold, often freezing temperatures of the highlands is a pleasure.

A wolf stalks its prey among the giant lobelia trees on the Sanetti Plateau.

The endemic Giant Mole-rat is the mainstay of the Ethiopian wolf diet. Since the mole-rat is at its most vulnerable above ground, it rarely strays more than a meter from its burrow entrance and is extremely good at reversing down its hole in the blink of an eye when faced with danger. It keeps one eye on the sky and one on its breakfast of sweet Lady's Mantle (*Alchemilla* genus).

As the sun sets a juvenile wolf scans the horizon for danger before he joins his pack for the night.

Following pages: The view from the top top of Tullu Demtu, the highest peak in the Bale Mountains.

Blick's grass rats may be the prey of the Ethiopian wolf, but it doesn't mean they aren't feisty and full of personality. They are also vocal, calling out warnings of approaching danger in voices far larger than expected from such a small animal.

Roughhousing among the pups helps to build the muscles and agility they will need to hunt.

Following Pages: Rocky terrain covered by low scrub brush is given an other-worldly appearance with the tall giant lobelia. These plants are one of the few that brave the strong, nearly constant winds that howl over the highlands.

THE ETHIOPIAN WOLF

social tendencies. They live in tightly knit packs, maintaining a clear hierarchy and ritualized greetings. All pack members help to raise new litters of pups and participate in patrols to defend the boundaries of their territory.

The Ethiopian wolf evolved to perfectly fit its habitat. It sits at the top of the food chain on the roof of Africa. Yet of the fourteen genera, and thirty-five species of canid in the world, the Ethiopian wolf also sits the farthest from safety. How is it that there are fewer than 450 members of the species left?

Several factors are at play. There is the continued loss of habitat to human encroachment and the ever-dwindling amount of prey resulting from overgrazing by herds of cattle and goats, which both trample and consume the vegetation the wolves' prey relies on. However, although these factors put the species in peril over the long term, the biggest immediate threat is the occurrence of two diseases that have been under control in the United States for decades: rabies and canine distemper virus. It is in part the tight social life of the wolves that makes these diseases such a serious problem.

A Very Social Life

Morning in the highlands is often welcomed with a layer of frost covering the scrub bushes and the coats of the wolves. But these hearty animals are built for this harsh environment. Their black noses appear from beneath their warm, thick tails, and as the sky brightens, the members of the pack stretch and yawn before standing to shake the frost from their dense fur and greet one another with warm affection.

During most of the year, the wolves of a pack sleep wherever they happen to meet up at the end of the day. A *Helichrysum* scrub makes a fine bed for a wolf. However, for four months in the autumn and early winter, the wolves gather and sleep each night in a rendezvous area near a den site as the next generation of wolves becomes the focal point around which pack life revolves.

Each morning, after spending some time stretching and bonding, the wolves set off to patrol their territory. This is one of the few times between dawn and dusk that the wolves move together as they follow the outline of their territory, renewing their scent markings and working together to repel any intruders they might encounter. Although the wolves of a pack are gentle and affectionate with one another, they can become aggressive when face to face with another pack, snapping and snarling to chase away any intruders. After all, it is a matter of life and death to have enough land with enough rats to feed all pack members.

Once the territorial border has been surveyed, the wolves veer off in individual directions to hunt their primary source of food: rats. A dozen rat species live in the Ethiopian highlands, ranging in size from the diminutive Blick's grass rat to the biggest prize, the endemic giant molerat. A wolf must eat four to five grass rats (typically 60-180 grams each) a day to sustain itself, or one giant molerat (which is much larger, weighing an average of 930 grams each). If you're the one stalking rats all day, you can quickly guess why a sizable mole rat is preferable whenever possible. Any additional food that a wolf catches is buried as breakfast for the following day or, during pupping season, is brought back to the den and shared with the dominant female and pups. Every member of the pack takes part in feeding the pups by sharing catches or staying behind to babysit while the dominant female goes to hunt.

The Hunt

Hunting a rat is a tough task. Rodents have keen hearing and swift reactions. That means the wolves must have even better hearing and faster reflexes. They use a plethora of techniques to catch their prey, the most common of which is directly stalking a rat. The wolf's large, sensitive ears catch the sound of a rat foraging near its

burrow. The closer it gets to the rat, the lower the wolf sinks to the ground, blending in with the surrounding brush. From this position the wolf can trot forward in short bursts, its belly just inches above the earth, resembling a rust-red arrow streaking over the ground. Eventually the wolf is close enough to pounce on the unsuspecting rat and, with luck, snatch it up in its long, slender snout.

But that certainly isn't the only option. Wolves will use rocks or bushes as cover to pounce on an unsuspecting rat or take a more direct course by digging the rodents out of their burrows. They will even follow passing herds of sheep, cattle, and horses, using the noise and bulk of the herd to conceal their approach, reaffirming the expression "wolf in sheep's clothing."

Even with this armory of hunting techniques, the wolves achieve only a 44 percent success rate in catching their prey. Luckily, there are approximately two tons of rodents per square kilometer of land, so there is always another chance to try the next hunting strategy.

In the late afternoon, the wolves seek one another out. They greet each arriving member with a range of vocalizations, from yip-like howls to whines and whimpers. The less dominant the pack member, the lower it holds its ears and tail on approach, but the joyful exuberance is barely contained. If you have ever seen a golden retriever greet his owner with the breed's signature full-body wiggle, you know the overwhelming joy the wolves exude upon finding one another. When the lip licking, sniffing, wiggling, and yipping is done, the wolves spread out to sleep, draping their faces in the warmth of their bushy tails.

It Takes a Pack to Raise a Pup

Every year between October and January, a special event occurs that brings the pack closer than ever and determines its future: the breeding season.

Because the successful rearing of a litter of pups requires the diligent efforts of every member of the pack, only the most dominant female will produce a litter. As the time for mating draws near, the female begins her flirtations. These include scent marking more often than usual, begging for food from the dominant male, and having a shorter temper with the lower-ranking females. Her primary mate is the dominant male of the pack. However, he may not be the only male with whom she mates. Genetic analysis of pups within litters shows that there may be multiple fathers to a litter of pups, which means the female will mate with the dominant male of her own pack as well as with males from outside of the pack. Because males typically stay within their natal packs for their entire lives, inbreeding is a real possibility. Having multiple partners is a way of maximizing genetic diversity and minimizing the chances of inbreeding.

Every so often, a less dominant female from the pack may also find a mate. If that happens, the litter of pups is not likely to come to full term. The pack can handle the needs of only one litter at a time, and subordinate females may be needed to help nurse the pups of the dominant female. Stress caused by the aggressive dominance displays of the alpha female are typically all that is required for the subordinate female to abort her pregnancy. Should she be successful in bringing her litter to term, the pups will likely be abandoned.

Approximately sixty days after mating, the female gives birth. In preparation, the female will enlarge an existing burrow or hollow or find a crevice set back in a rocky outcrop. It is here in this secluded den that she will give birth to and raise her litter of two to seven pups.

When born, the pups are blind and toothless, and their coats are a dark gray or black color. They won't gain the lighter brown coloring for another three weeks, or around the time when they emerge from the den for the first time. During those first fragile weeks, the pups stay hidden in the safety of the den and are entirely dependent on the female for milk.

When they are between three and four weeks old, the pups will have gained enough size and muscle strength to begin exploring the outside world. During their first few attempts to leave the den, they are just strong and brave enough to briefly peek out. But over the next four to six weeks they will become stronger by the day, as their milk diet is supplemented by meat regurgitated by other adults in the pack. To improve the chances of survival of the entire litter, subordinate females also may allo-suckle, even if they have never been pregnant before, providing additional sustenance for the growing pups. These short visits with adults outside the den turn into longer play sessions over the weeks, and eventually the play turns into practicing adult behaviors, such as stalking and pouncing.

When the pups are old enough to leave the den, they spend some time in the morning playing and bonding with the members of the pack. This is a vital time for the pups, when they learn social etiquette and practice hunting behaviors on one another (or on nearby rocks and blowing leaves). Eventually, they are encouraged back into the den so that the pack can begin the day's business of patrolling and hunting, with more play sessions sure to come later in the day, when the adults return.

Coming of Age

When they are around eight to ten weeks old, the pups are weaned off milk, and for the next several months they survive entirely on what meat the adults bring back for them. When an adult returns to the den site, the pups will run to greet it, gathering around and eagerly licking and smelling the adult's mouth. This helps trigger the regurgitation of a rat eaten shortly before, and the pups will quickly gobble down the scraps. Sometimes an adult may bring home a whole rat and drop it for the pups, who will promptly tear it to shreds in their scrambling for a piece of the prize. This sharing of food is vital for the youngsters, who have not yet grown big enough, let alone skilled enough, to hunt for themselves. The more adults in the pack, the more the pups will have to eat, increasing the likelihood that they will survive.

The pups continue to beg for food from adults until they reach the age of six months or a little older, after which their pleas will go unanswered. At that point they are considered to be old enough to hunt their own food and must perfect their hunting skills through daily practice. This is their time to gain full independence; the pups must move from being a burden to being a productive member of the pack. This period from six months to one year of age is the "trial by fire" for a wolf pup. If a pup does not learn to skillfully hunt, it will not make it into adulthood. Only about 50 percent of pups make it through this challenging period and into the next stage of their lives as sub-adults.

Between the ages of one and two years old, a wolf is considered a sub-adult. Nearly all sub-adult males stay with their natal pack, but the majority of females move off as "floaters" once they reach adulthood, most likely because they are driven out by the dominant female. Most females that leave their natal pack will disappear, meaning they leave the area under close scrutiny by the wolf watchers and are not seen again. They may join a pack that is not monitored by the researchers, or they may die where their carcasses are unlikely to be discovered. On rare occasions, some females form new packs with other floaters, male or female. This has happened only more recently, in response to the drastic reduction in wolf numbers resulting from disease outbreaks.

For example, when an outbreak of rabies hit the Meggity pack (one of the "focal" packs chosen for study and monitored by EWCP to understand the population changes among the species) it wiped out all but two females. Three males from the neighboring Alandu pack then joined them to form a new pack. Shortly afterward, a canine distemper outbreak hit, and only one male and one female survived. This pair is now all that is left of the Meggity pack which was once twenty-three members strong -- that is, except for the litter of four pups the pair had during the 2011 breeding season. All four juveniles are alive and healthy at this writing, and have just become sub-adults. The pack of six now has an even better chance at raising successful litters in the coming years. With such a small pack, the females may stay with their natal pack once reaching adulthood, to assist with raising new litters and defending their territory.

Of course, that is if everything works out perfectly for the pack. Pressures along its territorial lines are tough for the Meggity pack, because it has far fewer members to defend its hunting ground. For now, that is not a serious problem, because the small pack doesn't need as large an area for food as it once did. But should the pack grow back to its previous size, and hopefully it will, then it will have to rebuild its range.

However, Ethiopian wolf packs come into contact not only with rival packs, but also with two other species that are the cause of their plummeting numbers: humans and domestic dogs.

MEETING THE BBC PUPPIES

After nearly six weeks of camping in the highlands of Ethiopia, we had photographed the members of twelve packs. But we didn't yet have images of black-coated pups emerging from the den and seeing daylight for the first time. With only three days left in our trip, our last chance was the BBC pack, so named for the documentary crew that spent a season with it for the BBC "Islands in the Sky" documentary, the first film depicting wolf life on the roof of Africa.

Luckily, this pack is well habituated to humans. Rather than alarm calls from the adults, we were treated with a cursory glance and then complete indifference, which is exactly what we wanted.

We knew the dominant female of the BBC pack had given birth, but we weren't sure if the pups would emerge before we had to leave. Missing Christmas at home would land both of us in hot water so extending the trip wasn't an option. On the first day, we arrived in the early morning, but there was no activity around the den. Undaunted, we returned in the late afternoon around the time we expected the pack's wolves to return from hunting.

Our eyes strained as we scoured the landscape for any movement, then there she was, the dominant female, back from hunting. It went silent in the car, the cameras went up, and again, we waited, ready for anything that might indicate a pup making its first foray out from the dark den. The den was well hidden at the base of a hill, and it was difficult to keep an eye on exactly where it was, which bush it was under. The female went in, and finally—finally—tiny black ears poked up. The excitement in the vehicle was palpable. "Puppies!!"

Just one brave pup—its eyes barely open, its ears still folded forward—peeked out of the den that afternoon. We returned before sunrise the next morning with the hope that we would see all the pups emerge. The female came out about an hour after sunrise, and behind her came one, then another, then another and another. Squeals barely suppressed, we had tears streaming down our cheeks. It is difficult to contain one's emotions for something as significant, and as vulnerable, as the newborn of a critically endangered species.

With cameras clicking at full speed, we watched the pups tottering around like anamotronic puppets on their tiny legs. Eventually, perhaps twenty minutes later, the female decided it was enough exercise for the youngsters, and she took them back into their warm, dark den.

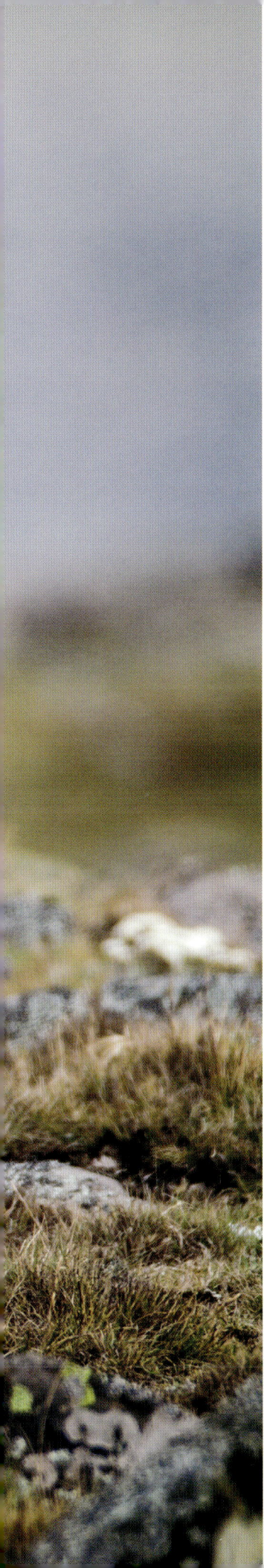

Standing as erect as a royal sentry, this wolf is on high alert, scanning the landscape for any sign of danger.

Each morning and evening, the wolves patrol the edges of their territory as a pack and remain alert throughout the day, especially when raising a litter of vulnerable pups.

Following pages: The bizarre rock formations of the Rafu Lava Flow remind us that the Bale Mountains were once a hotbed of volcanic activity.

A wolf from the Tarura pack catches forty winks during a quiet moment.

A toothy yawn is an opportunity to see the long narrow muzzle of the Ethiopian wolf, so perfectly shaped for catching rodents.

Ritualized greetings are a hallmark of Ethiopian wolf packs. They greet one another with diverse movements from joyfully wiggling bodies, to ears flattened in submission, to lip licking. The greetings are dependent on the status of the wolf within the pack, the more exuberant greetings given by the more submissive members.

Every member of the wolf pack pitches in to raise the young pups, including the alpha male who is no stranger to babysitting. The young pups demand almost constant attention, and while other pack members sometimes lose their cool and snap their teeth to display disapproval, the BBC male is always calm, patient and nurturing.

Following pages: Five members of the Tarura pack move fluidly across a frozen landscape in the Web Valley. Morning patrol is an important duty in which every pack member must participate. Each pack must be ready to defend its territory from neighboring packs and the richer the hunting ground, the more pressure a pack is under. Most borders are maintained by scent markings but occasionally packs will meet face to face and battles may ensue.

Pups from the Tarura pack in Web Valley greet the rising sun while mom takes advantage of their relative peace to clean an ear.

A rough and tumble game of pounce in the early morning frost is a favorite way to wake up and warm up when you're a wolf pup.

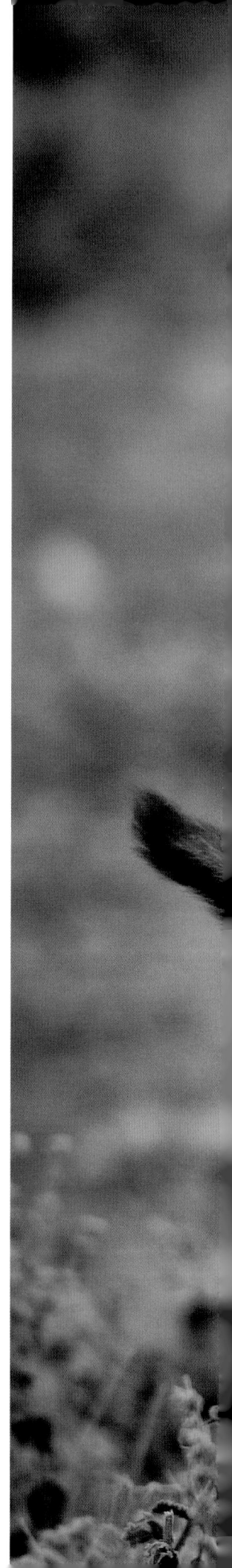

An afternoon of rowdy play between siblings works up a large appetite. The Meggity four seldom stopped for long but they always seemed to know when it was time for the adults to return with the spoils of their afternoon hunts. The high rocks above the den offered a good vantage point to rest and keep a look out.

A Shrinking Wolf Population

As is the case with many species, the presence of humans presents the wolf with a problem, or rather a complex web of problems. For wolves living near the herders on the Ethiopian highlands, the primary challenges include overgrazing by livestock and ground compaction, which alters the habitat of the wolves' main food source; loss of habitat and disruption from villages in the mountains; and proximity to unvaccinated dogs, which spread rabies and canine distemper virus. Currently, that last problem is the one most immediately and severely affecting the wolves.

As of this writing, only six small populations of Ethiopian wolves remain, with the largest population of about two hundred individuals living in the Bale Mountains. The remaining populations live in the Arsi Mountains, Simien Mountains, North and South Wollo, and Guassa-Menz, each of which holds anywhere from fifteen to seventy-five wolves.

Ethiopian wolves never were particularly abundant, even when they were first recorded. However, there is a big difference between the standard low population of an apex predator and a population dwindling to near-extinction numbers. With the former, the species can rebound after a bout with disease; with the latter, it can't.

Ethiopia currently has the fastest-growing human population in Africa, which means encroachment on wolf habitat for cropland and grazing land is increasing, and so is the frequency of contact between wolves and the disease-carrying dogs that live within

villages and move with herders. Proximity to villages and intensified contact with seasonal herders has hit wolf numbers hard.

Wolf populations are subject to cyclical crashes and recovery periods as diseases hit and packs rebound. But if a disease hits again before the pack has had a chance to recover its numbers, then it is more likely to wipe out the pack altogether. With the ever-increasing likelihood that a wolf will encounter an unvaccinated dog belonging to a herder, the length of time a pack has to recover from an outbreak is continually shrinking. For example, repeated rabies outbreaks among wolf packs occurred in the Bale Mountains in 1991, 2003, 2008, and 2009, and it was confirmed that the wolves had contracted the disease from domestic dogs. Outbreaks of canine distemper virus (CDV) in 2006 and 2010 in the Bale region of southern Ethiopia also did significant damage. As of 2011, 26 percent of adults and sub-adults in the Bale Mountains had died or disappeared during the previous twelve months, including the loss of six entire packs after the two rabies outbreaks in 2008 and 2009 and the CDV outbreak in 2010. The Bale population is the largest in the country and so has the resilience to rebound better from such a hit than other populations, but the one-two punch of a rabies outbreak immediately followed by a CDV outbreak is exactly the scenario that could end the species forever, should it happen again.

Even with the serious losses of the previous few years, forty-nine of the fifty-seven remaining packs in the Bale Mountains area still had a breeding pair of adults as of the end of 2011, which means that should enough packs successfully raise litters of pups, the numbers could bounce back—but only if all goes right for the wolves. The population of these wolves is tenuous at best. With fewer than 450 individuals remaining, the existence of the Ethiopian wolf in years to come is highly questionable. Unless steps are taken now to contain disease outbreaks, the photographs in this book may depict members of a species that may soon exist only in memory.

Highlands Herding Culture

The people of the Ethiopian highlands are primarily herders, tending to sheep, goats and cattle. Sheep win out as the most popular: a herd of seventy-five sheep (and a few goats for good measure) is both easier and cheaper to raise than a herd of cattle. The ease and frugality of keeping livestock are important features of their popularity, because these animals are not raised for slaughter, as one might expect. The animals in a herd are more a symbol of wealth than a source of food or even of income. The more animals one has, the more wealthy one is, even if those animals do not directly translate into food or products to sell in the market. Herders have very few material possessions, so it is their animals that establish their social rank.

The size of a herd is limited primarily by the cost of purchasing new animals. How many children a man has to tend the herd, as well as how far they can move the herd from village to grazing grounds and back are also factors affecting a herd's size. To oversimplify, even if resources are limited and a man is down to twenty sickly sheep, that's deemed more valuable than having five healthy animals, at least in the eyes of the herder.

The way most families generate an income is to bring goods to market. For the people of the highlands, goods include crops such as barley, onions, potatoes, cabbages, and other produce, and in some areas, such as Goba and other small towns surrounding

Bale National Park, firewood. In Goba, loads of wood are brought by donkey down to the villages and sold for fifty birr. For comparison, one cabbage is priced at one birr, or the equivalent of about sixteen U.S. cents. So a single load of firewood collected and sold can yield a significant bump to a families annual income. Once the wood is sold, a person can buy the food and other supplies needed to sustain a family or, more livestock.

The booming human population growth in Ethiopia is pushing people higher and higher into wolf territory in their effort to find enough space for herding and farming. And as the number of people rises, so too does the amount livestock. That is where both the short- and long-term trouble starts for the wolves.

Habitat Loss

For a relatively rare species that evolved to live only at high altitude, the extent to which its populations can range is very limited. With nowhere else to go, increasing encroachment by humans on its habitat is devastating.

Habitat loss is happening the world over as humans stretch farther into untouched natural areas, whether to convert those areas into cities or farmlands or to harvest resources such as timber, oil, or precious metals. No matter where or why it is happening, human encroachment into wildlife habitats leads to serious consequences. For the Ethiopian wolves, the loss comes from humans moving agriculture and grazing farther up the mountain slopes.

With people come roads and cars, overgrazing, den disturbance, bush fires, deforestation, and a range of other issues that lead to habitat fragmentation and disturbance, affecting everything from the abundance of prey to where and even when the wolves can hunt.

The wolves are daytime hunters. Their routine is to wake in the early morning, patrol as a group, split off to hunt alone all day, and return to the den site in the late afternoon. However, when more people move throughout their range, the wolves tend to become more secretive, hiding out during the day and hunting in the evening or at night. And there is one serious problem with switching to nocturnal hunting: the wolves' prey is mostly diurnal. If most rats are not out and active, the odds of catching enough of them to survive are slim. Still, some wolves are making it work. Those living in the Simien Mountains have started hunting species of nocturnal rats at dawn and dusk, and these species have become almost one-third of the wolves' diet. However, even with the seeming success of such changed habits, without sufficient foraging capabilities to sustain the pack, the wolves have a reduced chance of procreating or surviving in that area.

A more worrying change in behavior caused by human disturbance is that of switching dens. Conservationists have seen an increased loss of pups because the wolves are forced to move dens regularly in an effort to protect their litter. According to EWCP, the Garba Guracha pack located on the Sanetti Plateau lost all its pups during one breeding season because it moved dens three times in response to human disturbance. So although changes in feeding habits are problematic, the pressure to repeatedly move dens could be far more devastating.

There is no question among conservationists that the loss of wolf habitat is directly linked to the expansion of agriculture brought by the rising human population. The problem is rooted not only in what humans strip from the land, but also in how the land is divided. Habitat fragmentation is a serious problem for the wolves. It causes a loss in hunting range, increased contact with humans and their dogs, and population isolation, which limits genetic diversity. Fragmentation also means that the habitat can support only a smaller population of wolves, and smaller population size increases the risk of complete extinction for a pack or population that is hit by a disease outbreak.

Overall, the Ethiopian wolf currently has about 3,000 square kilometers of suitable habitat. The species can move only so high up the mountains, and right now agriculture is creeping upward, chasing the wolves to the limits of their livable habitat. Although 2,270 square kilometers of habitat lie within protected areas such as national parks, there is little to keep the wolves safe from villages set up within them.

For instance, a 2010 assessment of encroachment in the Bale Mountains National Park shows that more than 5,000 households, with more than 22,000 people and roughly 12,500 dogs, exist within this protected area. Encroachment has been a serious issue for years in the Simien Mountains National Park, where the numbers of livestock and subsistence farmers have continued to increase. In 2005, a survey found nearly 3,200 people living in 582 households within the park. Since then, the area of the park was increased, and although further settlement has been halted and grazing of livestock restricted, there are still about 30,000 people in thirty villages around the park and two within it. All told, there are some 4,650 cereal farmers living in and around the park, and perhaps as many herders, woodcutters, and others who use the area for their income. The resulting pressures on wolves living in these areas are immense.

Overgrazing and Ground Compaction

Habitat encroachment is problematic for the wolves not only because the presence of humans and livestock disturbs their hunting patterns, but also because the livestock literally change the face of their hunting range.

Goats and sheep are known the world over for their ability to eat just about anything, and that is no different in Ethiopia's highlands. When a herd comes through and clears an area of its vegetation, the rodent population dependent on that vegetation suffers. While some grazing is beneficial because it keeps an area clear enough for rodents to move about—for example, grazing naturally done by the endemic mountain nyala or the walia ibex—the introduction of livestock can quickly lead to a tipping point beyond which there is nothing left for the rodents to eat. With the subsequent drop in rodent populations comes trouble for the wolves.

Overgrazing has a partner problem as well: soil compaction. As livestock move over an area, their stomping hooves pack down the soil, collapsing existing burrow systems and making it harder for rodents to tunnel under the surface and move to new areas for food. It also makes it harder for seeds to take root, limiting the regrowth of vegetation. Abundant plant life is important not only to sustain the rodents but also to retain water and hold soil in place during rainstorms. Without it, rain washes over the barren area, taking topsoil with it and causing erosion that makes recovery for an area even more difficult, if not impossible.

The wolves are smart and have learned to use the herds to their advantage, at least sometimes. Following along behind them, they use the animals as cover for hunting

rodents. But that will offer little benefit over the long term, because the goats and cattle consume too much vegetation and destroy habitat of both rodents and wolves.

Scientific models show that the maximum livestock density at which rodents and wolves can survive in the Bale Mountains is between 32 and 117 head per square kilometer. When the number exceeds that, it is no longer sustainable for maintaining a healthy habitat. Right now, both the Web Valley and Morebawa—important wolf areas in the Bale Mountains—have an estimated density of 149 and 195 head per square kilometer, respectively, a density clearly too high for the wolves. Monitoring how many head of livestock are grazing per square kilometer is a way to identify areas experiencing the most trauma and perhaps help refine conservation strategies.

Domestic Dogs

In addition to the overgrazing and compaction of the earth by their herds, another more pressing problem has arrived with the humans. The closer humans come with their herds, the closer they bring their domestic dogs. It is these dogs, or more specifically the diseases they carry and spread, that are the most immediate cause of the downfall of the Ethiopian wolf.

The dogs are semi-feral, used more as an alarm system against leopards and spotted hyenas than as shepherds or pets. They are scruffy, with thick, matted fur and a sneaky, opportunistic temperament. They technically belong to the herder's family, but they remain at the edges of the group—close enough to be part of the family pack but not close enough to touch. So they are not cared for as pets or even as working animals—they are not spayed or neutered, nor are they vaccinated, and they are left to their own devices to find food and water. Unfortunately, that means they hunt the same rodent prey as the wolves, which brings the two predator species into contact and into competition with each other.

Coming close to infected dogs, or to the remains of infected animals, can mean death for not only one wolf but also the entire population in that area. Because the wolves live in packs and are highly social, if one picks up rabies while out hunting, the disease can spread through the entire pack in a matter of days. If that pack comes in contact with another pack during its morning patrol of territorial boundaries, then the second pack can catch and spread the disease just as quickly.

As an extraordinary example, the Meggity pack was eighteen members strong in 2008, but with one intense bout of rabies, it was reduced to two. The loss of sixteen wolves to rabies in such a short time is a serious blow to the species. In 1990 and again in early 1992, outbreaks of rabies devastated the Bale Mountains. The estimated wolf population was reduced from 440 down to 160 in a couple years underscoring the disease's alarming potential to wipe out a population and even the entire species in the blink of an eye.

Canine distemper can have the same impact on the wolf population. The disease wiped out one-quarter of adult and sub-adult wolves in the Bale Mountains population in 2010 alone. A loss of adults means a serious loss of pups as well. While monitoring focal packs, EWCP recorded that only three of the twenty-five pups born during the 2010 breeding season survived to the sub-adult stage, representing just a 12 percent survival rate. Losing pups and juveniles at such a high rate further reduces the chances of a population recovering after a disease outbreak.

In 1989, domestic dog density in the Web Valley was estimated at 0.7 dogs per square kilometer, or an average of 11 dogs per settlement. Dog numbers have undoubtedly grown as more people have moved into the mountains, and currently 20,000 dogs are estimated to live in and around the Bale Mountains National Park. The focal packs in the Web Valley studied by EWCP were hit hard first by rabies in 2008 and then by CDV in 2010. Now, four of the focal packs have died off and more than two-thirds of the adults and sub-adults disappeared.

Thankfully, the remaining three packs had a successful 2011-2012 breeding season and two new packs formed from floaters left without a pack after the outbreaks. But the closer in dogs move, the more difficult it becomes for the population to survive, let alone make a comeback.

In the United States, rabies has been effectively wiped out among domestic dogs, and CDV is under control in most areas, so there is little doubt of the potential for bringing the Ethiopian wolf back from its *Endangered* status through vaccination programs. However, that is far easier said than done.

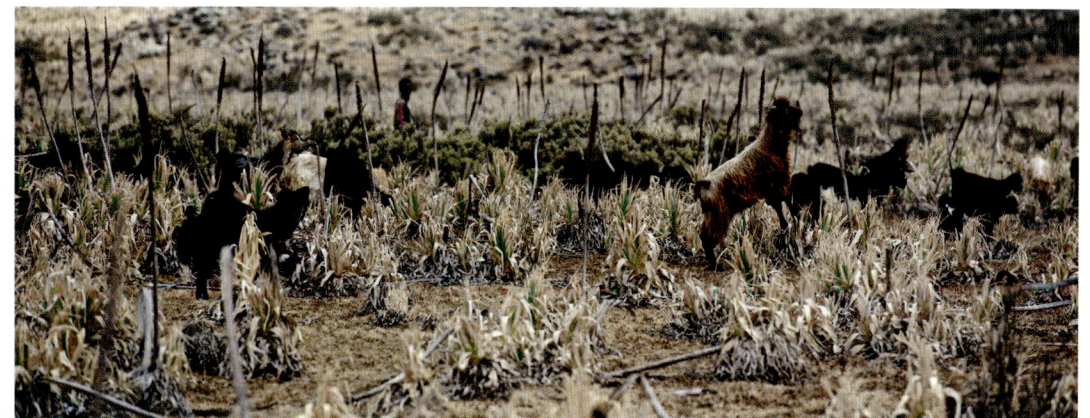

COFFEE CEREMONY

On our last day in Dinsho, a village within the boundaries of Bale Mountains National Park, our guide Musti invited us into his home to share in a coffee ceremony with his family. Although the ceremony is a part of the day-to-day life in Ethiopia, an invitation to join one is an honor and a mark of friendship. It was truly the best coffee we've had in our lives.

Coffee originated in Ethiopia and has spread across the entire world, but its preparation and sharing has maintained its original importance in Ethiopian culture. The ceremony begins with long grasses placed around the floor to bring the "freshness of nature" into the home. The host sits on a short stool while roasting the green beans to deep brown perfection, and everyone chats about the day's events. Fragrant incense such as frankincense or etan (gum Arabic) is often burned to chase away bad spirits, and it combines with the heavenly aroma of the roasting beans. We uttered heartfelt compliments such as *betam toruno* (lovely) as the smoke from the beans wafted toward us.

The roasted beans are ground by hand in a mukecha bowl with a zenezena stick (similar to a mortar and pestle) before being placed in the jebena (boiling pot). Popcorn is the accompanying snack of choice, and its salt helps to bring forth more of the rich flavors in the coffee. When it's finally ready, the coffee is poured into sini (small, handleless cups) from a great height through a filter of horsehair stuffed into the spout of the jebena. Some may spill, but that is a symbol of abundance, so no one worries over it. The first round is called *abol*, the second *huleutteunya*, and the third and most important is called *beureuka*, meaning "to be blessed." Each round is served by a young child of the house, with the first cup given to the eldest guest, or the most honored.

Amazing coffee shared over warm conversation with friends . . . life doesn't get much better than that. *Amesege'nallo'* Musti, *Ye bearakah bayt, ye seesigh bayt yahoon.* ("Thank you Musti, may He make this a blessed house and prosperous one.")

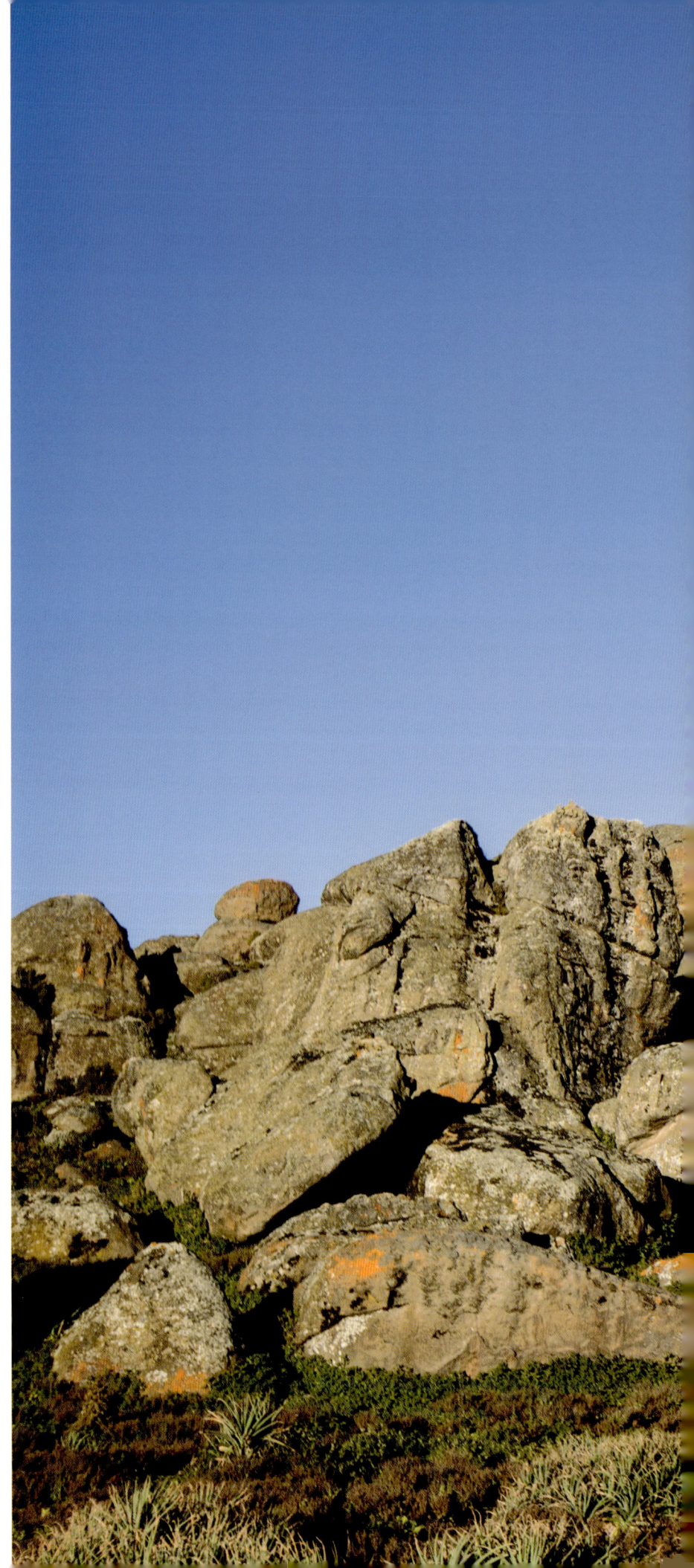

The traditional homes built of mud and wood blend perfectly into the landscape of the ancient Rafu Lava Flow.

This family of warthogs regularly visited our campsite in the Ethiopian highlands, so Will set up a remote camera with a wide-angle lens to photograph them as they rummaged around for food. They had just had a mud bath in some particularly red mud, hence their orange complexion.

This agile little klipspringer shows off the origin of his name while on guard duty. The literal translation in Dutch is "Rock Jumper".

Following Pages: While not nearly as high as Tullu Demtu, Mount Badagassa is an important landmark for navigating in the high Sanetti plateau where every dome can be seen from miles away.

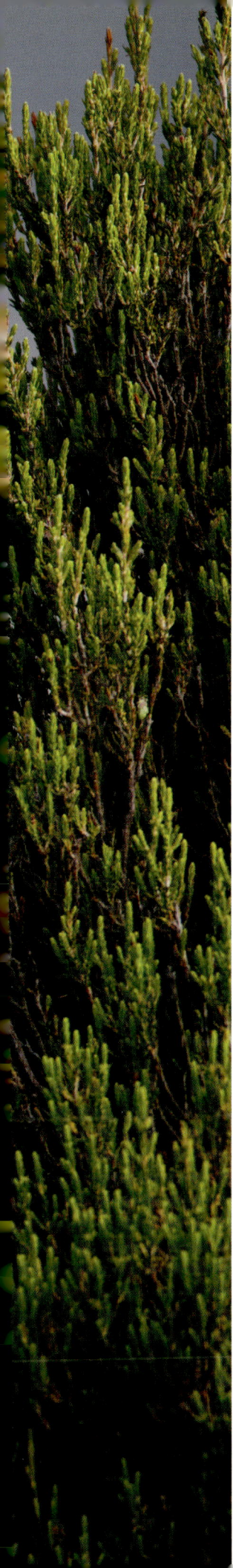

The Chestnut-naped francolin worries far more about predators flying above than predators with four legs. It's the raptors, not the wolves, that claim these birds as prey.

Blue-winged geese are endemic to Ethiopia and are just one of the several species of fowl found in the Ethiopian Highlands.

The rodents of the Bale Mountains aren't hunted by the wolves alone. Raptors like this Lanner Falcon congregate to take advantage of the rich rodent food source.

A male Mountain nyala pauses in the brush to check for danger.

The ubiquitous Olive baboon is as comfortable in the low Harenna Forest as it is high on the Sanetti Plateau, as pictured here.

The Abyssinian owl is perfectly camouflaged to its surroundings, making it quite a stealthy hunter of rodents.

Every so often a Starck's hare such as this one become's a wolf's prey.

CONSERVATION EFFORTS

Making a Difference

The Ethiopian Wolf Conservation Programme, established in 1988 by Claudio Sillero, has had a leadership role in studying the lives and needs of the Ethiopian wolf and in strategizing the best ways to protect the species based on sound science. The organization pours the maximal time, money, resources, and most importantly, optimism and dedication into the protection of these animals and the habitat in which they live.

Since its modest early days EWCP has grown significantly. The program currently employs more than thirty local Ethiopian staff and has hosted graduate students studying everything from wolf ecology and genetics to the relationships among overgrazing, rodents, and the wolves. The conservation programs EWCP has implemented over the years on behalf of the wolves may be the only reason why the species still exists today.

The organization's most important work, however, is that of building and implementing programs for vaccinating both dogs and wolves, thereby protecting the Ethiopian wolf as well as humans, their livestock, and domestic dogs from rabies and CDV.

The devastation caused by rabies among the Ethiopian wolf populations cannot be understated. The disease can wipe out entire packs in a matter of weeks or months. In 1990, more than half the wolves under study on the Sanetti Plateau were wiped out in just three months. Two years later, more than three-quarters of the wolves under study in the Web Valley were gone in just four months. In both 2003 and 2008, between 65 and 76 percent of the wolves studied in the Web Valley disappeared. In all cases, rabies was fingered as the culprit.

Let those numbers sink in for a moment. Imagine a population of wolves dropping from one hundred members to just twenty-five in a matter of months. Now think of the years it takes to rebuild the population to its former numbers, with each pack producing just two to seven pups a season, pups that may or may not make it to adulthood, and with the constant threat of another disease outbreak slashing its numbers yet again before it can recover. This is what the Ethiopian wolf is up against.

It is a similar story with CDV. In the Worgona Valley and Central Sanetti areas of the Bale Mountains, nearly half of all known wolves died or disappeared in 2005 and 2006, matching a 50 percent mortality rate of domestic dogs outside the Bale Mountains National Park from the disease. Later in 2010, some seventy-five wolves died or disappeared, with analysis of carcasses all testing positive for CDV. Another series of rabies or CDV outbreaks in one area, such as the Bale Mountains, may mean the extinction of the population in that area. This threat is both serious and likely, unless vaccination efforts are implemented quickly across the most important areas of wolf habitat.

Vaccinating Dogs

There are two approaches to keeping rabies and CDV out of wolf populations, and EWCP is working on both. The first is to vaccinate the semi-feral dogs that villagers use to protect their herds. The dogs are the species most likely to pass disease on to the wolves and other wildlife, so vaccinating them would create a buffer zone of vaccinated dogs around the wolves to protect them against outbreaks. The second is to vaccinate the wolves, a more direct course yet every bit as challenging in its own ways.

Dog vaccinations are a two-step process, entailing both the work that goes into vaccinating the dogs themselves, and the work that goes into educating the villagers about why vaccinations are so important. Due to the large numbers of dogs and

constant influx of new dogs from unchecked breeding, the vaccinations are provided on an annual basis. And without the support of the villagers, vaccinating so many animals is simply impossible.

Even with the full support of a village, vaccinating its dogs is a Herculean task. These semi-feral animals are not fed or even touched by the herders. Far from being pets, they are afraid of humans and often take off to the hills at the first sight of the EWCP veterinary team. However, the immense work of vaccinating these wary animals is well worth the effort, because vaccinations slow or even stop the spread of disease to the wolves, as well as to people and livestock. The dedicated EWCP veterinary team vaccinates more than four thousand dogs against rabies and CDV every year.

EWCP began vaccinating dogs in 1996, focusing on the Bale Mountains National Park, where the majority of wolves are located, and specifically beginning in Adaba Woreda, an area where dogs often move into the park and wolf territory. The program spread to other areas over the years, including the Simien Mountains and Guassa-Menz, North Shoa. EWCP has been able to make significant headway, vaccinating more than sixty-eight thousand dogs to date, predominantly in and around the Bale Mountains National Park.

While the program has been successful overall, there is one major hitch: a high turnover of dogs. New dogs are always arriving, coming in with the seasonal herders who inhabit the Bale Mountains for two months each year. These herders and their dogs pose as much of a threat to the wolves as those living in more permanent villages in the area, but they are harder to reach for vaccination efforts. Even so, the majority of dogs in the villages EWCP has worked with have been inoculated, and much of that is thanks to EWCP's efforts to clear up misconceptions about vaccinations.

In the past, villagers have been tentative about vaccinating their dogs. They worried that vaccination would make the dogs lazy and therefore less helpful as an alarm against predators and more dependent on village resources for their survival. Because these animals are meant for work, it would be a significant problem if they couldn't perform or were costly to keep. Luckily, educational programs have done a world of good in demonstrating to villagers that vaccinations actually keep their dogs healthier and therefore working for them longer. What's more, when villagers are educated on the positive benefits of rabies and CDV vaccination, they are far more likely to have their dogs caught and ready when the EWCP vet team arrives, making the vaccination process infinitely easier.

Inoculating dogs also means a drop in the number of rabies cases among humans and livestock. In villages where dogs have not been vaccinated, there is typically a 14.3 percent prevalence of rabies among humans, livestock, and dogs. That figure drops to just 1.8 percent for livestock and dogs in villages that have vaccinated their dogs, and the difference is even more profound when it comes to cases of rabies among humans: there is no occurrence of rabies at all among humans in vaccinated villages. By contrast, there is an 11.1 percent prevalence of rabies among humans in unvaccinated villages. Such a drop in the disease among humans alone is reason enough to promote vaccinating the dogs—as well as promote the use of the latest vaccines, rather than the ineffective and scientifically outdated ones currently used for humans in Ethiopia.

Of course, the benefits for humans and their animals are not the only reasons to vaccinate the dogs. Gathering support for protecting the Ethiopian wolf from disease and other threats is the ultimate goal of EWCP education programs, and that is where the next, and perhaps most important, part of the work with villagers comes into play.

Educating Local People

It takes a village to keep wolf populations safe. Or rather, it takes every village.

Because educational programs go hand-in-hand with vaccinating dogs, EWCP has made it a priority to bring them to as many villages as possible. The programs increase awareness of and support for rabies and CDV vaccinations, and they also boost understanding of how stewardship of an entire ecosystem plays a key role in keeping the habitats on which the villagers depend healthy and thriving. Awareness education has always been a primary tool for conservationists, and the more villages EWCP can reach, the more likely it is they will not only vaccinate more dogs the next time around, but also see progress in their sustainable use of the land.

EWCP has three full-time education officers, one in Bale Mountains region, one in Arsi Mountains region, and one who is responsible for the four northern wolf populations. The officers focus not only on raising awareness about the need for vaccinations, but also on the bigger conservation picture. In the schools, EWCP's educational campaigns emphasize environmental awareness and appreciation for natural resources, as well as the pressures currently imperiling the Ethiopian wolf and the importance of protecting the species. The education officers' campaigns are supplemented by EWCP's community officers, who work with village elders and women to extend the educational reach beyond the schools.

Within the eleven schools in the Bale area, EWCP reaches more than two thousand students and teachers each year. In Arsi, EWCP reaches more than eight hundred students and teachers in eight schools. Classroom activities include lessons about nature and conservation. Outside the classroom, students can participate in nature clubs and group projects in which they experience hands-on education, from planting trees to collecting litter. For example, Dinsho High School, in the Bale area, has a club called Experience Your Country, in which members visit the Bale Mountains National Park to enjoy the area and take part in educational activities. Students also learn to celebrate nature through the arts, such as participating in poetry competitions focused on the wolves and the threats facing them. Through this range of activities with schoolchildren, EWCP makes a connection with the minds of Ethiopia's future generation.

In Arsi, EWCP takes students on field trips to the mountains so they can see firsthand the wolves in their natural habitat. The power of seeing with one's own eyes the beauty of an animal, with a teacher who expresses the importance of and appreciation for that animal, cannot be overestimated. Now is a critical time to educate the students, because human disturbance is increasing in the habitats of the Arsi mountain range, especially through the burning of vegetation to make charcoal. Disturbingly, EWCP reports that two farmers admitted to killing two wolves in 2011. If students can bring to their families an excitement about and interest in the wolves and their well-being, it will give the species just a little more leverage in conservation efforts.

In the northern areas where four important wolf populations live, the education programs focus on this same strategy of appreciation for the wolves and the habitat the villagers share with them. Emphasizing coexistence and the sustainable use of resources, EWCP shows students how it is possible to protect the wolves and the future of the villagers' own land. The link between protecting the wolves and the preservation of the Afroalpine habitats on which a villager's family depends is a potent tool for shaping students into responsible stewards of the land. As they grow into adults, they are more likely to be advocates for the wolves and other endemic species as part of maintaining the health of their own resources, from grazing land to clean water.

Reaching beyond the schools in the Bale area, the education officer works with tourism guides in the National Park, teaching them more about the functions of the ecosystem, vital information that can be passed on to visitors. Additionally, EWCP holds annual celebrations such as World Rabies Day and EWCP Wolf Day, each of which features a bevy of festivities, including performances, art competitions, cultural displays, and games, all related to the appreciation of the wolves and their mountain highland habitat.

Vaccinating Wolves

The goals of EWCP are colossal. Keeping four thousand dogs vaccinated every year is in itself a monumental undertaking, especially given that the effort requires fundraising to buy vaccines; educating local people about the benefits of vaccinations, so they not only will allow the vet team access to their dogs, but also help catch the dogs before the team arrives; paying for the travel time and costs of the field teams; paying the three employees that it takes to vaccinate each dog; and more. At first glance, a more direct solution would seem to be to vaccinate the wolves themselves, because there are far fewer wolves than there are dogs. However, as is often the case, the most obvious path is not always the easiest to navigate.

The task of vaccinating the wolves is not nearly as straightforward as heading out to the highlands with some traps and a few vials of vaccine. When dealing with a critically endangered species, there is no room for error, as the Ethiopian government is keenly aware. While it is very supportive of EWCP's efforts to vaccinate dogs, the government is far more cautious when it comes to the wolves. It has allowed vaccinations in response to devastating outbreaks, and those measures were a significant success, stopping the spread of rabies, and essentially saving the species from extinction. But going ahead with any and every strategy with the potential for saving the wolves could turn disastrous through unintended consequences, so only the most well researched and proven plans have approval to move forward.

Of primary concern to the government is the type of vaccine to be used. The vaccine of choice in the US for controlling rabies in the coyote and raccoon populations has been a genetically modified oral vaccine. Ethiopia has strict regulations against genetically modified organisms (GMO) and GMO products, so another strategy is required. Also of concern is the stress caused to the wolves from annual capture and handling.

The next logical option is an oral attenuated live vaccine, which has been used successfully in bait drops in Europe to eradicate rabies in wild populations of red foxes. It has been tested on more than sixty species in the United States and Europe and has proven to be both effective and safe. The Ethiopian government has granted the EWCP permission to try this strategy one pack at a time. But even with government permission to proceed, barriers to success exist.

There is the challenge not just of getting bait to the majority of a pack, but also of ensuring the vaccine is properly consumed along with the bait. The vaccine is held within a packet hidden inside the bait, and that packet needs to be pierced so the vaccine can coat the mucus membranes in the wolf's mouth and be absorbed into the system. If the wolf doesn't pierce the packet, the vaccine won't be effective. Also, the wolf has to actually swallow the packet when it eats the bait. As any dog owner has experienced when trying to get a pet to swallow a pill hidden inside a treat, sometimes the treat goes down and the pill is expertly cast aside. The next series of trials will include more effective placement of the sachet to reduce the possibility that the bait will go down without the vaccine.

Another challenge is that, when not raising pups, individual members of a pack will cover miles of territory every day, sleeping wherever they happen to be when night falls and not returning to any specific location. Because of this roaming tendency, the best time of year to put out bait seems to be during pupping season, when the entire pack returns to the same den location day after day. That is the theory EWCP conservationists are currently testing, though the plan has a potential hiccup: the possibility that wolves will bring home bait to share as food, only to have a "bait monster" pup hog it all and neither the adult who brought the food to the den site nor the other pups receive the vaccine. Trials have shown that it is better to deliver the bait directly to an individual from horseback, rather than leaving baits near the den site.

Rabies vaccinations can last up to three years, but baiting would be done on an annual rotating basis, since there is no guarantee of getting doses to enough members of a pack during one round. In larger populations like Bale, forty percent of the members need to be vaccinated to ensure the survival of the pack while small populations would require upwards of 70 percent. The ideal would be for each individual wolf to consume at least one bait but no more than three in a single year. In reality, some wolves may never take a bait, while others eat more than their share.

Finally, the vaccine itself is not without its flaws. It must be stored below -30°C, because as it warms, it loses efficacy. Thus, the timing is critical for getting the vaccine from cold storage in the capital of Addis Ababa to the remote highlands where the wolves are found, many hours away, then into the bait, and finally into the wolves.

With all of these obstacles thoroughly researched and addressed, the EWCP was finally ready to begin a vaccination trial in 2011. Team members on horseback presented baits to the wolves. When a wolf took the bait, a team member recorded which wolf took it and how much bait was consumed. A few weeks later, it was time for testing the wolves to find out what percentage of the pack had been vaccinated and thereby determine the efficacy of the strategy.

In order to capture a wolf for testing, team members craft a tight horseshoe of bushes, which forces the wolf to enter at a specific spot to take a piece of bait staked down at the apex. Within this horseshoe, three traps are set in front of the bait. (They are rubberized leg traps, which cushion the wolf's foot from any damage beyond a possible bruise.) Once set, the traps are checked each hour. When a wolf is caught, two team members approach with a large blanket that they gently toss over the wolf. Just as a hood calms a falcon, the wolf becomes quite docile when faced with darkness, and the rest of the team is then able to approach. A reversible injectable anesthetic is administered to reduce the stress on the wolf from being handled, and the team goes to work.

This is not only an opportunity to test if the wolf has been effectively vaccinated, but also a perfect chance to check other vital information about the animal. Team members collect blood, tissue, and hair samples, take weight and length measurements,

and ear-tag the wolf. After the team works quickly to collect as much data as possible, the anesthetic is reversed, and the wolf runs off.

If EWCP can get even just 40 percent of a pack vaccinated for rabies, that can boost the pack's survival chances by as much as 90 percent. The pilot project by EWCP revealed that this strategy for administering the rabies vaccine is indeed effective, and now the organization is devising a disease control plan to protect all wolf populations against rabies.

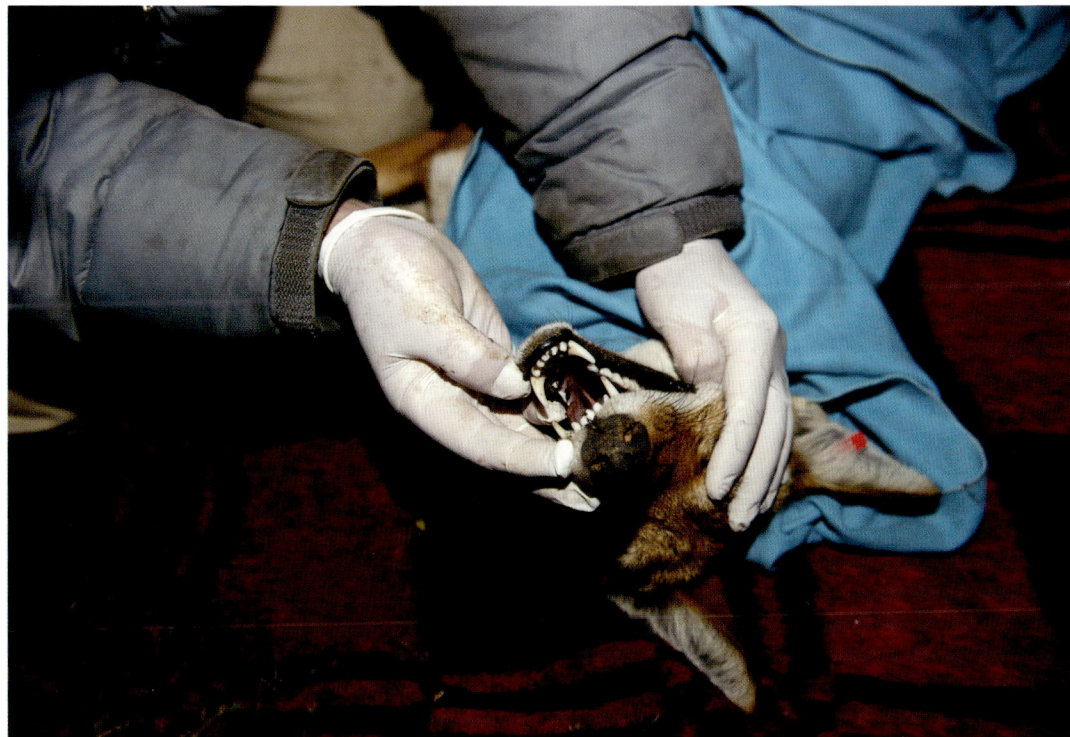

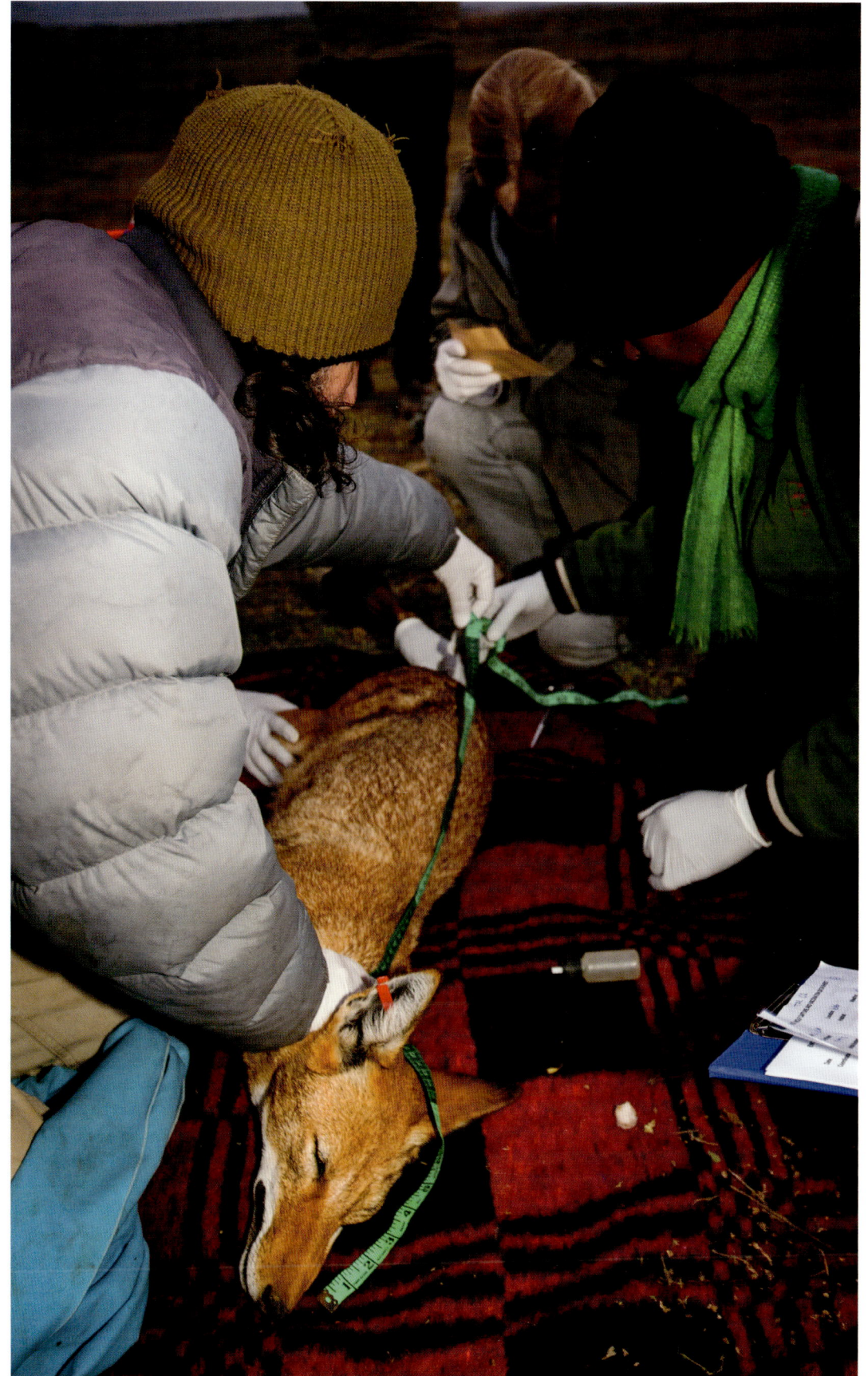

Behind the Scenes

PROPERLY STUCK

Getting good and stuck in the mud almost always starts with one mistake and gets worse with subsequent incremental mistakes. After a long night of rain, we piled into the truck at our usual 5:30 a.m. start time and wiped the fog from the front window. Will made his way along the route, by now well traveled. Our first mistake was not making sure we were able to see clearly through the front window, which kept fogging back over. The car's headlamps were tilted strongly to the left side, and the fog on the windshield prevented Will from seeing that the road was a bit darker green than normal after the rain.

We forged ahead and sure enough . . . spinning tires. No problem: we were halfway out of the mud anyway, nothing four-wheel drive can't handle if it's working, which apparently it wasn't. All of our usual tricks—putting mole rat dust, rocks, pebbles, and plants under the tires; rocking; digging—just made us sink deeper and deeper. An hour later, we had sunk the car right up to its undercarriage, broken our shovel, completely coated our poor guide, Muzeyen, with mud, and feared we wouldn't be able to pull the truck out without damage.

But Muzeyen would not give up. He marched off to camp, approximately a mile away, and shortly after marched right back with a new shovel, several long logs of firewood, our dear chef, Mamoush, and a pickaxe! It took six and a half hours of digging, rocking, and spinning tires before the truck finally rumbled back up the road into camp. There went a day of shooting, but a renewed respect for the persistence of Ethiopians!

We finally packed up all our gear and made it out of Web Valley in time to secure rooms in a hotel in Goba for the night while our beloved Toyota was in the shop to be fixed.

FOLIO FOUR

Preceding Pages: Giant lobelia trees (*Lobelia rynchopatelum*) appear as lone sentinels on the rim of the Web Valley.

Two pups from the Meggity pack spend the morning engaging in a lively game of King-of-the-Hill.

An adult from the Tarura pack stands on guard on a ridge amid fragrant sage plants (*Salvia* genus). There are few animals in the Bale Mountains that will take on a pack of Ethiopian wolves, but a spotted hyena, leopard or tawney eagle would make quick work of the small pups. To keep the litter safe, the pack patrols and keeps a close watch on its territory.

Following Pages: During patrol, the Tarura pack looks for any sign of intruders and refreshes scent markings along the edges of their territory.

A wolf pounces on its prey in an almost cat-like movement. Its long limbs and light body help it to stalk the rats, getting close enough to make one final jump to snatch up its prey.

Following Pages: Rafu is an area where an ancient lava flow has eroded to form a spectacular field of towering rock pinnacles. Each pinnacle can be over 10 meters (32 feet) high and the tightly packed formations extend far into the distance.

This little pup paused from his rowdy play to mimic mom for a moment as she scanned the valley below for any signs of trouble. It wasn't long before the little one was back to creating the trouble himself!

The rambunctious play of the wolf pups is important to their development. The rowdiness not only builds muscles but gives them practice for future hunting.

Following Pages: The BBC pack pups emerge from the den for the very first time in their lives. Though this initial foray into the world will be short, their play time outside the den will lengthen each day as they grow in size and strength.

133

Catch a wolf by the tail! As play builds hunting capabilities, it seems that this little pup will have no problem catching food in the future... as long as it has a tail!

Why should we care about saving the Ethiopian wolf from extinction? Most of the world doesn't even know this species exists, so why invest ourselves in the fight to save it when we have polar bears, pandas, and penguins to worry about—species that are already beloved in mainstream culture and in just as much need of protection?

Part of the answer comes down to one of the most intense and immediate problems across the African continent today: water. Ethiopia is the source of water for many of its neighbors and is often referred to as the "water tower" of eastern Africa. In the north, water from the highlands, including the Simien Mountains, feeds the Blue Nile River, one of the two major rivers feeding the Nile River and the source of most of its water and fertile soil. In fact, nearly 90 percent of the water and 96 percent of the sediment in the Nile River originates from Ethiopia, though not all arrives via the Blue Nile. Additionally, precipitation from the Bale region in the south of the country is the water source for Kenya and Somalia, primarily via the Dawa and Omo Rivers flowing into Kenya and the Shebelle and Jubba Rivers flowing into Somalia. More rivers feed neighboring Eritrea in the east and Sudan in the west. The care of the highlands is of tantamount importance for humans as well as wildlife – and the Ethiopian wolf is the iconic species that can help spur that stewardship.

Within Ethiopia itself, water from the highlands is critical for both domestic and agricultural use and for driving major aspects of the economy, including hydroelectric power and the mining interests expressed by China for minerals such as tantalum, which is used in transistors for mobile phones, computers, and similar electronics.

Water is a critical part of the mining process, used for everything from dust control to mineral processing, and the industry requires vast amounts. With so many uses dependent on the availability of water, and with the high risk of polluted water re-entering the groundwater system, stewardship of the water supply is vital for Ethiopia. The planet has seen too many examples of habitat and species loss as a result of misused water supplies. Struggles over water and land use by competing interests— from agriculture to industry to clean water for household use to what is needed to maintain healthy habitat for wild creatures—are not unique to the African continent where economic difficulties and resource scarcity are common. With many interests battling for the same limited supply, there are winners and losers. Most commonly the losers are the flora and fauna and the poorer portion of the human population. But the Ethiopian wolf lives in a country where a commodity as precious as water—and the habitats where that water runs—could be viewed differently, could be viewed with care and longevity in mind.

Ecotourism, a relatively new form of economic income for countries with amazing wild spaces and species, provides another powerful reason to protect the wolf and its habitat. Ecotourism has become popular as a way for people to travel the world while keeping a light environmental footprint, learning about the local wildlife, and sometimes even volunteering to restore habitat during their trip. Tourism in general and ecotourism in particular took off in Ethiopia as part of that global trend, and they are becoming a significant source of income for the country. In 2003, the Ecotourism Association of Ethiopia was founded, with a mission to promote Ethiopia's rich cultural heritage and its unique environmental features while also alleviating poverty and restoring environmental resources. As tourists eager to see the landscapes, wildlife and fading cultural history bring a steady flow of money to a growing nation, local

species and habitat are transformed into an economic asset, stimulating a passion to protect them. In addition, tourists coming to the country can see for themselves the richness of the highlands, developing a connection to the land and a drive to care for and preserve it.

Perhaps one of the most potent reasons to focus conservation efforts on the wolves is national pride. Protecting an endemic species is a symbol of a country's strength, forethought, and national pride, especially for a nation that has an unusual history in Africa: though it was occupied by Italy from 1936 to 1941, Ethiopia was never colonized by a European country. It is intensely proud of its independence and self-sufficiency. With such an uncommon history, it would be no surprise for Ethiopia to embrace its wolf, a species as unique to the African continent as the country itself.

While national economic and cultural interests stand out as incentives to protect the species, the importance of preserving the highlands and all its inhabitants is certainly not lost on the villagers living among the wolves. Those people with access to agricultural land understand and support the protection of natural resources, as a 2009–2010 study by Girma Eshete, a graduate student at Mekelle University, in northern Ethiopia, revealed through extensive interviews among villagers. They depend on healthy ecosystems, and they know it—and they know that the wolves are part of those ecosystems and an indicator of the overall health of the land. However, the support is not universal. Villagers who are literate, have larger herds, or live farther away from Afroalpine habitats are more supportive of conservation efforts than those who are illiterate, have smaller herds, or live closer to the ecosystems needing conservation. People living closer to the Afroalpine ranges often consider

certain wildlife problematic, sometimes even blaming wolves for livestock predation and rodents for crop destruction. Yet just over one-third of those interviewed in the survey still had a positive attitude toward the wolves, and 60 percent believed humans and wolves can coexist. Those are hopeful statistics, showing that educational programs like the ones EWCP runs can help bring villagers on board for conservation.

However, exactly how to educate highland villagers, as well as how to manage land in the highlands, are complex topics. Eshete's study also revealed that 87 percent of those interviewed wanted traditional management systems that are based on the availability of water and grasses in the lowlands and highlands according to the seasons, a strategy that is beneficial to preserving the habitat as the rotation helps prevent overgrazing. However, 91 percent also wanted community-led, not government-led resource management systems for conservation. That could pose a problem because with a rapidly growing human population in its habitat, the Ethiopian wolf must be protected in recognized, controlled, and patrolled conservation areas. Even if a community has the best of intentions to sustainably manage the land, human needs will undoubtedly come first. Government regulations may better serve the wolves, even if those regulations do not precisely follow the preservation strategy preferred by villagers. The wolves need significant advances in protection, however they come about, and the best protection comes with programs that balance the needs of both the wolf and human populations.

One community-based effort that is managing to have a positive effect is the Habitat Change Project, started by EWCP and the Frankfurt Zoological Society in 2009. This project looks at the consequences of habitat encroachment for cropland and grazing land and the possible solutions that could limit or even reverse the resulting damage. It also looks at the impacts of climate change on the highlands and the trend of cropland extending farther up into the mountains as temperatures warm. Taking into account both the needs of the wolves and the needs of the Ethiopian people, the project attempts to find balance so that both can continue to survive. After all, protecting the habitat means protecting the livelihood of the people, including their grazing land, firewood, thatching grass and other construction materials, clean water, and medicinal plants, not to mention tourism. Encouraging villagers to participate in conservation efforts will bring positive benefits to them far beyond bringing wolves back from near extinction.

The presence of an apex predator is evidence of a healthy ecosystem; without the foundations of healthy soil, vegetation, and herbivore populations, a habitat cannot support carnivores high on the food chain. Just as the presence of sharks on ocean reefs or wolves in the forests of North America indicate a balanced ecosystem, so too does the presence of the Ethiopian wolf in the highlands. Indeed, through a carefully constructed chain, including natural systems, economics, and human culture, the Ethiopian wolf is closely linked to the water supply, livelihood, and even identity of eighty-five million people living downstream.

Luckily for this species, the Ethiopian wolf is an ideal animal to act as an emblem for conservation. Much as the polar bear is a compelling figure whose survival as a species

brings awareness of the perils of climate change, the Ethiopian wolf is a beautiful and dynamic species with which many people can feel a connection. After all, they are cousins of our own canine companions. Nearly 40 percent of Americans own at least one dog, and consumers spend an average of fifteen hundred dollars a year on their dogs, proving that canids are close to our hearts. That feeling of connection and appreciation can foster interest in habitat conservation for the survival of the Ethiopian wolf.

As much as their appearance and location, it is the wolves' behavior that inspires conservationists. The wolves build a village—they work as a group to protect their territory, they all help to raise each litter of pups, they take care of their pack mates, and will even share their extra food among the pack. There's a beauty to that, and a lesson to be learned. It takes effort to create and care for a community, and these wolves embody that ideal. By helping one another, they are our mentors for improving our planet.

Preserving from extinction a charismatic wolf that exists in only one place in the world, that doesn't pose a threat to humans or livestock, that is elegant and lively, leads an admirable social life, and truly has a hope of being saved? This would be a wonderful and inspiring conservation achievement to share with our next generation.

A LAST MEAL

Our final morning with the BBC pack had us wondering how much trouble we would be in if we stayed one more week and arrived home late for Christmas. In the end we decided five weeks and two broken cameras were enough, and it was time to travel home.

As we watched the pack leave on its morning patrol, we were well pleased with the range of behaviors, ages, and environments we had captured. The only shot we were missing was a good rodent capture.

We turned the vehicle toward camp, our minds beginning to wander to the hot shower we knew awaited us in Dinsho that night. Suddenly the dominant female appeared at the side of the road, as if she had been waiting for us to show up. She waited patiently as we maneuvered to the side of the road and pulled out our cameras. Then, certain she had our full attention, she turned, gave a quite confident look over her shoulder as if to say, "Check this out," and pounced. Success!

She lifted a large grass rat into the air and dispatched it with ease. Then she proceeded to show us every angle of the rat before consuming it. Another look clearly told us, "Now you can put the cameras away."

HOW YOU CAN HELP

The Ethiopian wolf needs your support and by purchasing this book you've already begun to help. Proceeds from *Hope at the Edge of Extinction* are being donated to the Ethiopian Wolf Conservation Programme. This money will be used to purchase life-saving vaccines, equipment to keep wolf monitors working effectively and safely in the field, to fund education programs and much, much more.

It doesn't stop there! You can visit the following organizations to make direct donations to help save these beautiful creatures and their highland habitat. Thank you for supporting the wolves.

ETHIOPIAN WOLF CONSERVATION PROGRAMME (EWCP)
WWW.ETHIOPIANWOLF.ORG

WILDLIFE CONSERVATION NETWORK (WCN)
WWW.WILDNET.ORG
TWITTER: WILDNETORG

BORN FREE FOUNDATION
WWW.BORNFREE.ORG.UK
WWW.BORNFREEUSA.ORG
TWITTER: BFFOUNDATION

WILDLIFE CONSERVATION RESEARCH UNIT (WILDCRU)
WWW.WILDCRU.ORG

ETHIOPIAN WOLF PROJECT
WWW.ETHIOPIANWOLFPROJECT.COM
TWITTER: EWPROJECT

ACKNOWLEDGEMENTS

SPECIAL THANKS for help with the realization of the Ethiopian Wolf Project:

Our Kickstarter Supporters
Maureen Baboolal, Donna Bloomquist, Jon and Victoria Bonney, Megan Burrard-Lucas, Natalie Burrard-Lucas, Sandia and Stephen Burrard-Lucas, Terence Burridge, TC Chew, Sophie Core, Lee Crawley, Beate Dalbec, Brian Doerfler, Chris Drew, Alice Dryden, Dianna Edgar, Matthew Edgar, Bruce Finocchio, Amy Flood, David Gill, Edie Howe-Byrne, Madelyn and Jerry Jackrel, Matthew James, Haje Jan Kamps, Doug King, David Lloyd, Dylan Madeley, Kate Messina, Kristan Norvig, Peter Norvig, Alexander Pay, Richard Peters, Ian Powell, Ruta Rakutis, Carolyn and David Rogers, Monica Samec, Bonney Schermerhorn, Porter Schermerhorn, Miriam Schulman, Ian Solberg, Kathy Tonegawa, Sarah Treanor, Tonya Vokral, Dairian Wan, Peter Ware and MD88.

The Staff of the Ethiopian Wolf Conservation Programme
Dr. Claudio Sillero, Anne-Marie Stewart, Chris Gordon, Edriss Ebu, Mustafa "Musti" Dule, Muzeyen Turkee, Alo Hussein, Leta Idea, Zegeye Kibret and all of the wolf watchers, veterinary staff, education officers and guards who work every day to help the Ethiopian wolf survive.

The Staff and Volunteers of the Wildlife Conservation Network especially Kelly Wilson.

Charles Harris, Dan Suzio, Enrique Aguirre and Michelle Gilders for their support and indispensable advice.

The Sufu Marketing team of Susannah Fuidge and Tom Hadley for all the help spreading the word.

From Will: Thank you to Nat and my parents, Sandia and Steve for always supporting me.
From Rebecca: Warm thanks to Lee for always meeting me at the airport with a grin and our dog.
From Jaymi: Thank you, April, for smiling and nodding at every new idea and over-sized project I launch into.

SINCERE APPRECIATION goes out to all the authors listed in the reference section. Your work, words and stories helped us immeasurably in understanding the story of the Ethiopian wolf.

IMAGE LIST

REFERENCES
BOOKS

Carillet, J., Butler, S., Starnes, D. (2009). Ethiopia and Eritrea. London: Lonely Planet Publications Pty Ltd.

Crossette, B. & Kollodge, R. (2011). UNFPA State of World Populations 2011. New York: United Nations Population Fund.

Hunter, L. (2011). Carnivores of the World. New Jersey: Princeton University Press.

Kebede, T. (2008). Ethiopian Ahmaric. Victoria: Lonely Planet Publications Pty Ltd.

Kingdon, J. (1989). Island Africa, The evolution of Africa's rare animals and plants. New Jersey: Princeton University Press.

Lohan, T. (2010). Water Matters: Why we need to act now to save our most critical resource. San Francisco: AlterNet Books.

Macdonald, D.W., & Sillero-Zubiri, C (2004). Biology and Conservation of Wild Canids. Oxford: Oxford University Press.

Pol, J.L.V. (2001). A guide to endemic birds of Ethiopia and Eritrea. Addis Ababa: Shama Books.

Reading, R., Miller, B. (2000). Endangered Animals, A reference guide to conflicting issues. Westport: Greenwood Press.

Scardina, J., & Flocken, J. (2012). Wildlife Heroes: 40 leading conservationist and the animals they are committed to saving. Philadelphia: Running Press.

Tamene, M., Bekele, A. (2012). Human-wildlife conflict in the Simien Mountains National Park. The case of Ethiopian wolf and gelada baboon. Saarbrücken: Lambert Academic Publishing.

Yilma, A. (2009). The impact of vaccinating dogs against rabies and its prevention in human, livestock and dogs in selected Peasant Associations of Bale Zone. A thesis submitted to the College of Veterinary Medicine, Mekele University, Ethiopia.

WEBSITES
Marino, J. & Sillero-Zubiri, C. 2011. Canis simensis. In: IUCN 2011. IUCN Red List of Threatened Species. Version 2011.2. <www.iucnredlist.org>. Downloaded on 03 April 2012.

"Rabies Fact Sheet." World Health Organization. < http://www.who.int/mediacentre/factsheets/fs099/en/>. September 2011.

"Oral Rabies Vaccine Information." United States Department of Agriculture, Animal and Plant Health Inspection Service. < http://www.aphis.usda.gov/wildlife_damage/oral_rabies/rabies_vaccine_info.shtml>. Updated: Aug 15, 2012.

Parry, Vivienne. "Why fear of vaccination is spelling disaster in the developing world." The Guardian. < http://www.guardian.co.uk/lifeandstyle/2010/oct/11/vaccination-fears-developing-world-deaths>. (accessed July 2012).

"The oral vaccination of foxes against rabies." Directorate General for Health and Consumers - European Commission. < http://ec.europa.eu/food/fs/sc/scah/out80_en.pdf>. (accessed June 2012).

"Industry Statistics and Trends of Pet Ownership." American Pet Products Association. < http://www.americanpetproducts.org/press_industrytrends.asp>. (accessed: July 2012).

ARTICLES

Gottelli, D., Sillero-Zubiri C., Applebaum D., Roy M. S., Girman D. J., Garcia-moreno J., Ostrander E. A., and R. K. Wayne. 1994. Molecular genetics of the most endangered canid: the Ethiopian wolf Canis simensis. *Molecular Ecology* 3: 301-312.

Gottelli, D., Marino, J., Sillero-Zubiri C. and Funk, S.M. (2004), The effect of the last glacial age on speciation and population genetic structure of the endangered Ethiopian wolf (Canis simensis). *Molecular Ecology*, 13: 2275–2286. doi: 10.1111/j.1365-294X.2004.02226.x

Knobel, D. L., Fooks, A. R., Brookes, S. M., Randall, D. A., Williams, S. D., Argaw, K., Shiferaw, F., Tallents, L. A. and Laurenson, M. K. (2008), Trapping and vaccination of endangered Ethiopian wolves to control an outbreak of rabies. *Journal of Applied Ecology*, 45: 109–116. doi: 10.1111/j.1365-2664.2007.01387.x

Malcolm, J. 1997. The diet of the Ethiopian wolf (Canis simensis Ruppell) from a grassland area of the Bale Mountains, Ethiopia. *African Journal of Ecology* 35: 162-164.

Mech, David. "The Scientific Classification of Wolves: Canis lupus soupus." *International Wolf*, Spring 2011.

Rueness EK, Asmyhr MG, Sillero-Zubiri C, Macdonald DW, Bekele A, et al. (2011) The Cryptic African Wolf: Canis aureus lupaster Is Not a Golden Jackal and Is Not Endemic to Egypt. PLoS ONE 6(1): e16385. doi:10.1371/journal.pone.0016385

Sillero-Zubiri, Claudio. "Unraveling the Biogeography of Wolf-like Canids in the Horn of Africa." *International Wolf*, Winter 2011.

Asefa Deressa; Abraham Ali; Mekoro Beyene; Selassie, B. N.; Yimer, E.; Kedir Hussen. (2010) The status of rabies in Ethiopia: A retrospective record review. *Ethiopian Journal of Health Development* 2010 Vol. 24 No. 2 pp. 127-132. www.cih.uib.no/journals/EJHD

D.T.Haydon, D. A. Randall, L. Matthews, D. L. Knobel, L. A. Tallents, M. B. Gravenor, S. D. Williams, J. P. Pollinger, S. Cleaveland, M. E. J. Woolhouse, C. Sillero-Zubiri, J. Marino, D. W. Macdonald & M. K. Laurenson. (2006) "Low-coverage vaccination strategies for the conservation of endangered species." *Nature* 443, 692-695 -12 October 2006

Sillero-Zubiri, C. and D. Gottelli. 1994. Canis simensis. Mammalian Species 485: 1-6.

Tallents, L. A., Randall, D. A., Williams, S. D. and Macdonald, D. W. (2012), Territory quality determines social group composition in Ethiopian wolves Canis simensis. Journal of Animal Ecology, 81: 24–35. doi: 10.1111/j.1365-2656.2011.01911.x

Ginsberg, J. R. and D. W. Macdonald. 1990. Foxes, Wolves, Jackals, and Dogs: An action plan for the conservation of canids. Canid Specialist Group and Wolf Specialist Group, the World Conservation Union, Gland, Switzerland.

Sillero-Zubiri, Claudio and D. W. Macdonald. 1997. The Ethiopian Wolf: Status Survey and Conservation Action Plan. IUCN/SSC Canid Specialist Group, Gland, Switzerland and Cambridge, UK.

Sillero-Zubiri, Claudio, Hoffman, Michael and D. W. Macdonald. 2004. Canids: Foxes, Wolves, Jackals and Dogs: Status Survey and Conservation Action Plan. IUCN/SSC Canid Specialist Group, the World Conservation Union, Gland, Switzerland and Cambridge, UK.

IUCN/SSC Canid Specialist Group. 2011. Strategic Plan for Ethiopian Wolf Conservation. IUCN/SSC Canid Specialist Group, produced at the strategic planning for Ethiopian wolf conservation meeting in Lalibela, Ethiopia.

Marino, Jorgelina. 2012. Ethiopian Wolf Conservation Programme: Habitat Change Project Annual Report. University of Oxford, UK.

Stewart, A.M., Gordon, C., Marino, J. and Sillero-Zubiri, C. (2012) Ethiopian Wolf Conservation Programme: Annual Report. Ethiopian Wolf Conservation Programme, Dinsho Bale, Ethiopia.

Gordon, C., Marino, J., Stewart, A.M. and Sillero-Zubiri, C. (2011) Ethiopian Wolf Conservation Programme: Annual Report. Ethiopian Wolf Conservation Programme, Dinsho Bale, Ethiopia.

Stewart, A.M., Gordon, C. and Marino, J. (2010) Ethiopian Wolf Conservation Programme: Annual Report. Ethiopian Wolf Conservation Programme, Dinsho Bale, Ethiopia.

Hemson, G. (2009) Ethiopian Wolf Conservation Programme: Annual Report. Ethiopian Wolf Conservation Programme, Dinsho Bale, Ethiopia.

Hemson, G. (2008) Ethiopian Wolf Conservation Programme: Annual Report. Ethiopian Wolf Conservation Programme, Dinsho Bale, Ethiopia.

Malcolm, J. (2007) Ethiopian Wolf Conservation Programme: Annual Report. Ethiopian Wolf Conservation Programme, Dinsho Bale, Ethiopia.

Malcolm, J. (2006) Ethiopian Wolf Conservation Programme: Annual Report. Ethiopian Wolf Conservation Programme, Dinsho Bale, Ethiopia.

Sillero-Zubiri, C. (2005) Ethiopian Wolf Conservation Programme: Annual Report. Ethiopian Wolf Conservation Programme, Dinsho Bale, Ethiopia.

Williams, S. (2003) Ethiopian Wolf Conservation Programme: Annual Report. Ethiopian Wolf Conservation Programme, Dinsho Bale, Ethiopia.

Williams, S. (2001) Ethiopian Wolf Conservation Programme: Annual Report. Ethiopian Wolf Conservation Programme, Dinsho Bale, Ethiopia.

Gordon, C., Marino, J., Stewart, A.M. and Sillero-Zubiri, C. (2010-2011) Ethiopian Wolf Monitoring Report. Ethiopian Wolf Conservation Programme, Dinsho Bale, Ethiopia.

Gordon, C., Hussein, A., Marino, J., Stewart, A.M. and Sillero-Zubiri, C. (2011-2012) Ethiopian Wolf Monitoring Report. Ethiopian Wolf Conservation Programme, Dinsho Bale, Ethiopia.